Thank You God

Psalm 145:5

I will think about your wonderful works.

Psalm 18:49

I will sing praises to your name.

Psalm 7:17

I will give thanks to the LORD.

Psalm 56:3

I will trust in you.

Psalm 31:7

I will rejoice in your love.

Psalm 86:7

In the day of trouble I will call to you.

Psalm 56:4

I will not be afraid.

Psalm 123:1
I lift my eyes to you.

Hebrews 8:12

I will keep my tongue from sin.

Psalm 27:6

I will make music to the Lord.

Psalm 71:15

I will tell of your goodness.

1 John 4:14

Thank you for sending your Son to be
the Saviour of the world.

Psalm 119:8

I will obey your commands.

Psalm 4:8
I will lie down and sleep in peace.